# italian breads

# italian breads
*from focaccia to grissini*

with recipes by
Maxine Clark

RYLAND
PETERS
& SMALL

LONDON NEW YORK

**Designer** Iona Hoyle
**Commissioning Editor** Julia Charles
**Production Controller** Toby Marshall
**Art Director** Leslie Harrington
**Publishing Director** Alison Starling

**Indexer** Hilary Bird

First published in the
United Kingdom in 2009
by Ryland Peters & Small
20-21 Jockey's Fields
London WC1R 4BW
www.rylandpeters.com

Text © Maxine Clark,
Linda Collister, Liz Franklin 2009
Design and photographs
© Ryland Peters & Small 2009

ISBN: 978 1 84597 899 0

10 9 8 7 6 5 4 3 2 1

A CIP record for this book is
available from the British Library.

Printed in China

Notes
• All spoon measurements given
are level unless otherwise specified.
• Eggs used are medium unless
otherwise specified.
• All dough rising times given are
approximate as they will depend on
the consistency of the dough and
the ambient temperature. There
may also be slight variants in
water quantities depending on
the humidity and the absorption
qualities of the flour being used.
• Ovens should be preheated to
the specified temperatures. All
ovens work slightly differently.
We recommend using an oven
thermometer and suggest you
consult the maker's handbook for
any special instructions, particularly
if you are cooking in a fan-assisted
oven, as you will need to adjust
temperatures according to
manufacturer's instructions.

# contents

# introduction

Nothing smells as good as freshly-baked bread still warm from the oven. Baking your own at home is a hugely enjoyable and satisfying process – with basic ingredients, simple equipment and the recipes given in this book, you will be able to make a variety of delicious Italian-style loaves and rolls to enjoy every day.

The main ingredients necessary to make Mediterranean-style breads are flour, salt, yeast and water, though they are often enriched with flavoursome ingredients such as olives, nuts or dried fruits. Choosing the right flour is important for a good result. Throughout Italy, *Farina de Grano Tenero* is used for breadmaking – this is the finest, whitest grade of soft wheat flour. '0' indicates the grade of the flour – '00' being the finest. Do shop around to find it.

Yeast is available fresh or dried and it's really up to you which you prefer to buy. Whatever yeast you use, it needs moisture and warmth to develop. Make sure the liquid is at the correct temperature – too cold and the dough will rise slowly; too hot and you risk killing the yeast. When a recipe states 'hand-hot water' it should be between 40.5°C (105°F) and 46°C (115°F). Also, the softer the water, the better the dough, so I like to use filtered or bottled water. Breads, such as focaccia, rely heavily on olive oil for their flavour, so do use extra virgin olive oil. It need not be an expensive one – most supermarket blends are fine.

As far as equipment goes, you should have a good selection of mixing bowls, measuring spoons, measuring jugs, weighing scales and a sharp knife or pastry wheel for cutting dough. My favourite gadget is a pastry scraper which can be used as a knife, scoop and board scraper. A steady work surface at the right height is essential for energetic kneading. This surface should be able to cope with sticky dough, flour and olive oil and be easy to clean. A flour shaker is also useful; an olive oil pourer will let you drizzle small amounts of oil; and a water spray mists dough with just enough water to keep it moist and is essential kit.

For baking, you will need deep, heavy metal tins for deep-pan focaccias, heavy rectangular tins for larger loaves and good, heavy rimless baking trays for pizzas and flatbreads. Tins with a non-stick surface tend to 'stew' doughs so I prefer to use metal, iron or heavy aluminium. Some recipes suggest using a testo – this is a type of bakestone that is heated in the oven for at least 30 minutes before starting to bake and mimics the base of a real pizza oven. When the uncooked dough comes into contact with the stone, the moisture is absorbed and the heat evenly distributed. It's a worthwhile investment if you intend to make a lot of pizzas and flatbreads but a sturdy baking tray will also do the job. So roll up your sleeves and start bread-making today – once you've tasted your own loaves I guarantee you'll never want to buy lack-lustre supermarket bread again!

# loaves and rolls

This is almost an Italian equivalent of garlic bread, but much better. You can use ordinary pizza dough, or enrich it with egg. The thin dough base is smothered in pesto and green olives, rolled up to look like a long Swiss roll and left to rise again. Drenched in garlic oil and smothered in pecorino cheese, the smell alone wafting from the oven is to die for!

# rolled pesto, olive and garlic bread

500 g Italian '00' flour or plain white flour

1 teaspoon sugar

½ teaspoon fine sea salt

25 g fresh yeast, 1 tablespoon dried active yeast or 2 teaspoons fast-action dried yeast

1 egg, beaten

3 tablespoons extra virgin olive oil

350 ml hand-hot water

250 ml fresh pesto

200 g large green olives, stoned and roughly chopped

200 g freshly grated pecorino or Parmesan cheese

2–3 tablespoons garlic-infused olive oil

sea salt and freshly ground black pepper

*a rimless baking tray*

*a terracotta bakestone or a large, heavy baking tray*

makes 1 medium loaf

Sift the flour, sugar and salt into a large bowl and make a well in the centre. Crumble in the fresh yeast or sprinkle in the fast-action dried yeast, if using. If you are using dried active yeast, follow the manufacturer's instructions. Rub in the yeast until the mixture resembles fine breadcrumbs. Pour in the beaten egg, olive oil and hand-hot water and mix until the dough comes together. Knead the dough energetically on a floured work surface for 5 minutes until soft, smooth and elastic. Put it in a lightly-oiled bowl, cover with clingfilm or a damp tea towel and leave to rise in a warm place until doubled in size – about 1½ hours.

Preheat the oven to 200°C (400°F) Gas 6. Put the bakestone or heavy baking tray in the oven to heat up.

When risen, knock back the dough, then roll or pull into a large rectangle as thinly as you can, directly onto a sheet of non-stick baking paper. Spread the dough liberally with the pesto, leaving a 1-cm rim all around the dough, then scatter over the olives and 125 g of the pecorino. Season. Using the baking paper, roll the dough up like a Swiss roll, starting from the long side. Slide the dough onto another sheet of baking paper making sure the seam is underneath. Brush with the garlic oil and sprinkle with the remaining pecorino.

Slide the rolled bread onto the rimless baking tray. Working quickly, open the oven door and slide both paper and bread onto the hot bakestone or baking tray.

Bake in the preheated oven for 20 minutes, then carefully slide out the baking paper. Bake for a further 5 minutes until the crust is golden. Remove from the oven and serve warm (not hot) or cold in slices.

This is an unyeasted bread from Umbria, and very quick to rustle up. When making this type of bread, work quickly, because as soon as the liquid comes into contact with the baking powder, a chemical reaction starts to aerate the bread. Use a light hand and get the dough into the oven as soon as possible.

# Parmesan soda bread

300 g Italian '00' flour or plain white flour

1 teaspoon baking powder

1 teaspoon fine sea salt

50 g freshly grated Parmesan cheese, plus extra to dust

50 g butter, melted and cooled

100–150 ml milk

2 eggs

a testo, terracotta bakestone or a large, heavy baking tray

a rimless baking tray, lined with non-stick baking paper

makes 1 medium loaf

Put the testo, terracotta bakestone or a large, heavy baking tray on the lower shelf of the oven. Preheat the oven to 190°C (375°F) Gas 5 for at least 30 minutes.

Sift the flour, baking powder and salt into a medium mixing bowl. Stir in the Parmesan and make a well in the centre.

Whisk the cooled, melted butter with 100 ml of the milk and the eggs, and pour into the well. Mix until just combined – overmixing will make the bread tough. The dough should be quite soft; if it isn't, add a little more milk. Turn out onto a floured work surface and knead briefly. Put the ball of dough directly onto a rimless baking tray lined with non-stick baking paper. Pat into a disc about 3 cm thick. Brush with a little extra milk, then mark into wedges with the back of a knife and dust with Parmesan.

Working quickly, open the oven door and slide paper and bread onto the hot testo, bakestone or baking tray. If you are brave, try to shoot the bread into the oven so that it leaves the paper behind – this takes practice!

Bake for 15 minutes, then very carefully slide out and remove the baking paper. Bake for a further 5 minutes or until the crust is really golden. Remove from the oven and wrap in a clean tea towel. Serve warm, broken into wedges, ready to split and fill.

This is a simple yet delicious rustic loaf flavoured with fresh sage. It is particularly good served warm from the oven and is the perfect accompaniment to hearty winter soups and stews. It works particularly well with pumpkin or butternut squash dishes as the musky sage complements their sweetness perfectly.

# Tuscan fresh sage and olive oil bread

375 g plain white flour

125 g plain wholemeal flour

2 teaspoons freshly chopped sage leaves

1 tablespoon baking powder

½ teaspoon fine sea salt

2 large eggs

3 tablespoons olive oil

about 175 ml milk

a baking tray, lightly greased

makes 1 medium loaf

Preheat the oven to 180°C (350°F) Gas 4.

Mix the flours with the chopped sage leaves, baking powder and salt in a large bowl.

In a separate bowl, lightly beat the eggs with the olive oil and milk, then stir into the dry ingredients to make a soft and slightly sticky dough. If there are dry crumbs or the dough feels stiff, work in a little more milk.

Turn out the dough onto a lightly-floured work surface and shape into a ball about 18 cm across. Put it on the prepared baking tray and score the top with a sharp knife.

Put in the oven immediately and bake for about 45 minutes or until golden brown and the loaf sounds hollow when tapped underneath with your knuckles. Transfer to a wire rack and leave until cool enough to break into quarters or cut into thick slices. This loaf is best eaten the same day but can be frozen for up to 1 month.

variation:
To make an Olive and Rosemary Bread, follow the same method as above, replacing the sage with 1 teaspoon freshly chopped rosemary needles and adding 75 g roughly chopped stoned black and green olives.

Ciabatta comes from Northern Italy and has become almost as popular and ubiquitous as the baguette. It has a floury crust, a moist open texture and a good flavour of fruity olive oil. For the best results, use an Italian ciabatta flour, which is granular and quite coarse in texture. This helps create a lively dough producing the large air bubbles needed for the characteristic texture.

# ciabatta rolls

300 ml hand-hot water

15 g fresh yeast*

500 g ciabatta flour or unbleached strong white bread flour

2 teaspoons fine sea salt

4 tablespoons extra virgin olive oil

For the biga (aged-dough starter):

250 g unbleached strong white bread flour

5 g fresh yeast*

150 ml hand-hot water

2 baking trays, heavily floured

makes 12 rolls

* If using fast-action dried yeast, mix one-third of a 7 g sachet with the flour to make the biga, then work in the water. Finish the biga as in the main recipe. To make the ciabatta dough, add the water to the biga and work in to make a batter. Then mix half the flour with one 7 g sachet of fast-action dried yeast, add to the batter, and finish as in the main recipe.

To make the biga, put the flour in a large bowl and make a well in the centre. Crumble the yeast into the well, then pour in the hand-hot water. Mix the yeast with the water, then gradually work in the flour to make a firm dough. Turn out onto a lightly-floured work surface and knead for 2 minutes, then return the dough to the bowl and cover. Leave at room temperature for 8–12 hours – it will rise enormously, then fall back.

The next day, to make the ciabatta dough, put the hand-hot water in a bowl and crumble the yeast over the top. Stir well until dispersed. Add to the biga and work into the dough by stirring and squeezing with your fingers to make a thick, smooth batter. Work in half the flour to make a very sticky, batter-like dough, then beat with your hand for 5 minutes until the dough has been thoroughly stretched and become very elastic. Cover the bowl and leave to rise in a warm place until about 2½ times its original size, about 2 hours.

Add the salt and olive oil to the dough, then gradually work in the rest of the flour to make a rather soft, sticky dough. When the dough feels smooth and very elastic, cover the bowl and leave to rise in a warm place as before, this time until doubled in size, about 1 hour.

Preheat the oven to 230°C (450°F) Gas 8. Put the baking trays in the oven to heat up.

Gently tip the dough onto a well-floured work surface. Using a floured bread scraper, divide the dough into 12 pieces and transfer to the trays, spacing well apart. Shape into rough-looking rolls with well-floured fingers. Dust heavily with flour, then slip the trays into large plastic bags, slightly inflated. Leave to rise in a warm place for about 30 minutes until almost doubled in size – don't worry if the dough also spreads out. Uncover the rolls, then bake in the preheated oven for 15–20 minutes, until golden brown. Cool on a wire rack. Eat warm from the oven or within 1 day.

These are delicious little savoury rolls made just like Chelsea buns and baked together in a tin. Take the whole lot to the dinner table and break off your own little roll. Perfect with drinks on a warm summer's night, or instead of bread – they will disappear very fast!

# walnut and parsley rolls

1 recipe Basic Pizza Dough (page 18)

200 g walnut pieces

a large handful of fresh flat leaf parsley leaves

2 garlic cloves

100 ml extra virgin olive oil

sea salt and freshly ground black pepper

*a deep pizza pan or springform cake tin, 23 cm diameter, lightly oiled*

makes about 20 small rolls

Preheat the oven to 200°C (400°F) Gas 6.

Put the walnuts, parsley and garlic in a food processor and process until evenly chopped. While the machine is running, pour in the olive oil. Season to taste.

Uncover the dough, punch out the air and roll or pull it into a rectangle, 60 x 20 cm, directly onto a large sheet of non-stick baking paper.

Spread the walnut mixture evenly over the dough. Season with salt and pepper. Using the baking paper, roll the dough up like a Swiss roll, starting from the long side. Slide the dough onto another sheet of baking paper making sure the seam is underneath. Using a large and very sharp knife, cut the roll into 20 even pieces. Cut the dough quickly and smoothly each time – don't saw it or it will stick! Arrange the rolls cut-side up in the prepared pizza pan, spacing them close together but not quite touching. Cover with clingfilm or a damp tea towel and leave to rise in a warm place for 30 minutes, until the dough has risen to the top of the pan.

Remove the clingfilm and bake the rolls for 35–45 minutes or until golden. Leave to cool in the pan if you want them very soft, or turn them out onto a wire rack to cool if you'd like them drier. Serve warm.

Having a recipe for a good basic pizza dough is essential. This will make the typical Neapolitan pizza base – soft and chewy with a crisp crust or cornicione, or it can be used as the basis of a number other recipes throughout the book. I find 250 ml water usually works for me, but if your flour has been kept in dry conditions, it may need a drop more to make a soft dough.

# basic pizza dough

25 g fresh yeast, 1 tablespoon dried active baking yeast or 2 teaspoons fast-action dried yeast

½ teaspoon sugar

250–300 ml hand-hot water

500 g Italian '0' flour or unbleached strong white bread flour

1 teaspoon fine sea salt

1 tablespoon olive oil

makes 2 medium-crust pizza bases, each 25-30 cm diameter

In a medium bowl, cream the fresh yeast with the sugar and whisk in the hand-hot water. Leave for 10 minutes until frothy. For other yeasts, follow the manufacturer's instructions.

Sift the flour and salt into a large bowl and make a well in the centre. Pour in the yeast mixture, then the olive oil. Mix together with a round-bladed knife, then use your hands until the dough comes together. Tip out onto a lightly-floured work surface, wash and dry your hands, then knead the dough briskly for 5–10 minutes until smooth, shiny and elastic – 5 minutes for warm hands, 10 minutes for cold hands! Don't add extra flour at this stage – a wetter dough is better. If you feel the dough is sticky, lightly flour your hands, not the dough. The dough should be quite soft. If it is really too soft, knead in a little more flour.

To test if the dough is ready, roll it into a fat sausage, take each end in either hand, lift the dough up and stretch the dough outwards, gently wiggling it up and down – it should stretch out quite easily. If it doesn't, it needs more kneading. Shape the dough into a neat ball. Put it in an oiled bowl, cover with clingfilm or a damp tea towel and leave to rise in a warm place until doubled in size – about 1½ hours.

Uncover the dough, punch out the air, then tip out onto a lightly-floured work surface. Divide into 2 and shape into smooth balls. Place the balls well apart on non-stick baking paper, cover loosely with clingfilm and leave to rise in a warm place for 60–90 minutes. Use as required.

# focaccia and flatbreads

The word focaccia means a bread baked directly on the hearth, and derives from the Latin word for 'hearth' (focus). Although a rustic focaccia can be made with any basic pizza dough, the secret of a truly light, thick focaccia lies in giving the dough three risings, and dimpling the dough so that it traps olive oil while it bakes.

# deep-pan focaccia

750 g Italian '00' flour or plain white flour

½ teaspoon fine sea salt

25 g fresh yeast, 1 tablespoon dried active yeast or 2 teaspoons fast-action dried yeast

150 ml extra virgin olive oil

400–450 ml hand-hot water

coarse sea salt or rock salt, to sprinkle

fresh rosemary sprigs (optional)

*2 cake tins, pie or pizza pans, 25 cm diameter, lightly oiled*

makes 2 deep focaccias

Sift the flour and fine sea salt into a large bowl and make a well in the centre. Crumble in the fresh yeast, or add the fast-action dried yeast, if using. If you are using dried active yeast, follow the manufacturer's instructions. Pour in 50 ml of the olive oil, then rub in the yeast until the mixture resembles fine breadcrumbs. Pour in the hand-hot water and mix together with your hands until the dough comes together.

Tip the dough out onto a floured work surface. Wash and dry your hands and knead the dough energetically for 10 minutes until smooth and elastic. The dough should be very soft. Put the dough in a lightly-oiled bowl, cover with clingfilm or a damp tea towel and leave to rise in a warm place until doubled in size – about 1½ hours.

Uncover the dough, punch out the air and divide into 2. Shape each piece into a round ball on a lightly-floured work surface and roll out into two 25-cm circles and place in the tins. Cover with clingfilm or a damp tea towel and leave to rise in a warm place for 30 minutes.

Preheat the oven to 200°C (400°F) Gas 6.

Uncover the dough. Push your fingertips into the dough right down to the base of the tin to make deep dimples all over the surface. The dough will deflate slightly. Drizzle very generously with olive oil (about 80 ml). Sprinkle with coarse sea salt and top with sprigs of rosemary (if using). Re-cover with clingfilm or a damp tea towel, put in a warm place and leave the dough to rise to the top of the tins – about 30 minutes.

Spray the focaccias with water and bake in the preheated oven for about 20–25 minutes, until risen and golden. Drizzle with the remaining olive oil, then transfer to a wire rack to cool.

Eat on the same day or leave to cool, then wrap up and freeze. When you remove the focaccia from the freezer, thaw and wrap in foil, then reheat for 5 minutes in a hot oven.

This is a wonderful example of the traditional focaccia, as it is baked directly on the bakestone or on a hot baking tray. If the base is floured very well the focaccia can be slipped directly onto the stone or baking tray, leaving the baking paper behind. This is the kind of focaccia that you tear and dip into yet more fruity olive oil.

# thin focaccia

1 recipe Deep-Pan Focaccia (page 21), risen twice but uncooked

100 ml extra virgin olive oil

coarse sea salt or rock salt, to sprinkle

*2 testi, terracotta bakestones or large, heavy baking trays*

*2 rimless baking trays, lined with non-stick baking paper*

makes 2 large, thin focaccias

Put the 2 testi, terracotta bakestones or large, heavy baking trays on the lower shelf of the oven. Preheat the oven to 220°C (425°F) Gas 7 for at least 30 minutes.

Uncover the dough, punch out the air and divide into 2. Shape each piece into a rough ball, then pull and stretch each ball of dough to a large oval shape – as large as will fit in your oven. Put each one on a rimless baking tray. Cover with lightly-oiled clingfilm or a damp tea towel and leave to rise for 30 minutes.

Remove the clingfilm and, using your fingertips, make deep dimples all over the surface of the dough right down to the baking tray. Drizzle over all but 2 tablespoons of the remaining oil. Spray the focaccias with water and sprinkle generously with coarse sea salt. Working quickly, open the oven door and slide the paper and focaccia onto the hot bakestones or baking trays.

Bake for 15 minutes, then very carefully slide out and remove the baking paper. Bake the focaccia for a further 15 minutes or until the crust is golden. Brush or drizzle with the remaining olive oil, then transfer to a wire rack to cool.

Eat on the same day or leave to cool, then wrap up and freeze. When you remove it from the freezer, thaw and wrap in foil, then reheat for 5 minutes in a hot oven.

Use this spicy focaccia to make delicious sandwiches or serve it in thick slices spread with cool, fresh ricotta. Replacing some of the liquid in the dough with tomato purée (or even all the water with tomato juice) gives it a beautiful, rusty red colour, studded with bright red pepper and dark chunks of salami or chorizo.

# fiery focaccia

½ recipe Deep-Pan Focaccia (page 21), making the changes stated in this recipe

4 tablespoons tomato purée

4–6 red chillies or Peppadews, diced

2 red peppers, roasted, deseeded and diced

100 g salami or chorizo, cubed

75 g provolone, Emmental or Gruyère cheese, cubed

100 ml extra virgin olive oil, plus extra to glaze

coarse sea salt or rock salt, to sprinkle

freshly ground black pepper

*a cake tin or pizza pan, 25 cm diameter, lightly oiled*

makes 1 focaccia

Make the focaccia dough following the recipe on page 21, but using 4 tablespoons tomato purée dissolved in the water. Knead the dough and give it the first rising.

Uncover the dough, punch out the air and pull or roll it out into a rough circle. Dot with the chillies, red peppers, salami, provolone and lots of freshly ground black pepper. Flip one half of the dough over and lightly knead to incorporate the ingredients. Shape into a rough ball on a lightly-floured surface and pat into the prepared tin. Cover lightly with clingfilm or a damp tea towel and leave to rise in a warm place for 30 minutes.

Remove the clingfilm and, using your fingertips, make deep dimples all over the surface of the dough. Drizzle over the olive oil, re-cover very lightly with clingfilm and leave to rise for a final 30 minutes until very puffy.

Preheat the oven to 200°C (400°F) Gas 6.

Uncover the focaccia, spray with water and sprinkle generously with coarse sea salt. Bake for 20–25 minutes, until risen and golden. Transfer to a wire rack, brush with olive oil and leave to cool.

Eat on the same day or leave to cool, then wrap up and freeze. When you remove it from the freezer, thaw and wrap in foil, then reheat for 5 minutes in a hot oven.

This is an unusual bread from the coastal areas of Lunigiana, made from a mixture of cornmeal and wheat flour. It is traditionally made between November and the end of January to coincide with the olive harvest and cooked in a wood-fired oven on a bed of chestnut leaves. I had some on a recent visit there – my friend's boyfriend made it in a bread oven outside on the terrace.

# cornmeal and olive focaccia with rosemary and sage

500 g Italian '00' flour or plain white flour

300 g fine polenta flour (*farina gialla* or *granoturco*)

two 7-g sachets fast-action dried yeast

200 g black olives, stoned and halved

3 tablespoons pine nuts

2 tablespoons freshly chopped sage

2 tablespoons freshly chopped rosemary needles

2–3 garlic cloves, finely chopped

3 tablespoons extra virgin olive oil, plus extra to drizzle

450 ml hand-hot water

coarse sea salt or rock salt, to sprinkle

freshly ground black pepper

*a Swiss roll tin, 33 x 23 cm, oiled*

makes 1 large focaccia

Mix the flours and yeast in a large bowl. Add the olives, pine nuts, sage, rosemary and garlic, then mix. Make a well in the centre and add the olive oil mixed with the hand-hot water. Mix to a very soft dough, turn out onto a lightly-floured work surface and knead very vigorously for 10 minutes.

Roll or pull the dough into a rectangle to fit the Swiss roll tin, pushing the dough into the corners. Cover with clingfilm or a damp tea towel and leave to rise in a warm place for about 20–30 minutes until quite puffy.

Preheat the oven to 200°C (400°F) Gas 6.

Using your fingertips, make deep dimples all over the dough and drizzle with olive oil. Sprinkle with coarse sea salt and grind over some black pepper. Bake for about 35 minutes, until risen, firm and dark golden.

Eat on the same day or leave to cool, then wrap up and freeze. When you remove it from the freezer, thaw and wrap in foil, then reheat for 5 minutes in a hot oven.

Making a bread by mixing mashed potato with flour and anointing it lavishly with good olive oil is common all over Italy, especially in Liguria and Puglia, where some of the best olive oil comes from. It is delicious, but quite dense. I tend not to stone the olives for this as they can dry out too much in the oven but don't forget to warn whoever is eating it before serving.

# potato and olive focaccia

500 g floury potatoes (such as King Edwards, Golden Wonder or Kerr's Pinks), unpeeled

600 g Italian '00' flour or plain white flour

½ teaspoon fine sea salt

25 g fresh yeast, 1 tablespoon dried active yeast or 2 teaspoons fast-action dried yeast

200 g large, juicy green olives, with stones in

150 ml extra virgin olive oil

coarse sea salt or rock salt, to sprinkle

*2 cake tins, 25 x 4 cm, or a large rectangular roasting tin, lightly oiled*

makes 2 medium focaccias

Boil or bake the potatoes in their skins and peel them whilst still warm. Mash them or pass them through a potato ricer.

Sift the flour with the fine sea salt into a large bowl and make a well in the centre. Crumble in the fresh yeast, or add the fast-action dried yeast, if using. If you are using dried active yeast, follow the manufacturer's instructions. Add the potatoes and mix together with your hands until the dough comes together. Tip the dough out onto a floured work surface, wash and dry your hands. Knead the dough energetically for 10 minutes until smooth and elastic. The dough should be soft; if it isn't, add a couple of tablespoons of warm water.

Divide the dough into 2, shape each piece into a round ball on a lightly-floured surface and roll out into two 25-cm circles or a large rectangle to fit whichever tins you are using. Put the dough in the tins, cover with clingfilm or a damp tea towel and leave to rise in a warm place for 2 hours.

Preheat the oven to 200°C (400°F) Gas 6.

Uncover the dough, scatter over the olives, and, using your fingertips, make deep dimples all over the surface of the dough, pushing in some of the olives here and there. Drizzle with 100 ml of the olive oil, re-cover and leave to rise for another 30 minutes.

Uncover the dough, spray with water and sprinkle generously with coarse sea salt. Bake for 20–25 minutes until risen and golden brown. Brush or drizzle with the remaining olive oil, then transfer to a wire rack to cool.

Eat on the same day, or leave to cool, then wrap up and freeze. When you remove the focaccia from the freezer, thaw and wrap in foil, then reheat for 5 minutes in a hot oven.

When I was teaching in Italy, I made focaccia in all shapes and sizes, and with many different flours. I wondered how it would taste if I incorporated my native oatmeal. I decided to use fine oatmeal and '00' flour and to scatter porridge oats and salt on top. The result was a thin, crisp, but still moist focaccia, with a golden, crunchy topping.

# oatmeal focaccia

2½ teaspoons dried active yeast

1 teaspoon sugar

350–450 ml hand-hot water

125 g fine oatmeal, warmed

500 g Italian '00' flour or plain white flour, warmed

2 teaspoons English mustard powder

1 teaspoon freshly ground black pepper

2 teaspoons fine sea salt

2 tablespoons extra virgin olive oil, plus extra to drizzle

3–4 tablespoons porridge oats

coarse sea salt or rock salt, to sprinkle

*2 Swiss roll tins, 23 x 32 cm, oiled*

makes 2 thin focaccias

Whisk the yeast and sugar into the hand-hot water and stir in the warmed oatmeal. Cover and leave to stand in a warm place for 10–15 minutes until frothy.

Sift the flour, mustard powder, pepper and fine sea salt into a warm bowl, pour in the oatmeal mixture and add the olive oil. Mix to a soft dough. Add a little extra warm water if the dough looks too dry. Turn out and knead for at least 10 minutes or until elastic.

Place in a lightly-oiled bowl, cover with clingfilm or a damp tea towel and leave to rise in a warm place for about 1 hour or until doubled in size.

Uncover the dough, punch out the air and divide into 2 pieces. Pull and roll each piece to fit the Swiss roll tins. Put in the tins and press into the corners. Prick the dough all over with a fork and scatter the porridge oats and coarse sea salt over the top. Cover with oiled clingfilm or a damp tea towel and leave to rise in a warm place until puffy – about 30–60 minutes.

Preheat the oven to 200°C (400°F) Gas 6.

Drizzle the focaccia with olive oil and bake for 25 minutes, until golden. Remove from the oven and drizzle with a little more olive oil. Cool on a wire rack and serve cut into thin fingers. Best eaten the same day.

In Italy these flatbreads are known as piadine (a piadina is a 'little plate') and are traditionally cooked on a testo (a thick, flat piece of terracotta). As these are difficult to buy outside Italy, I use unglazed terracotta plant-pot saucers with great success. Never oil a testo – it must be clean and dry. Keep the piadine warm and soft inside a folded napkin in a basket until they are ready to serve. Serve them warm, folded over, with thinly sliced prosciutto or salami piled inside.

# flatbreads from Emilia Romagna

500 g Italian '00' flour or plain white flour

1 teaspoon baking powder

a pinch of fine sea salt

4 tablespoons good olive oil, melted unsalted butter or pure lard

200 ml hand-hot water

a testo, iron girdle or heavy-based frying pan

makes about 8 flatbreads

Sift the flour, baking powder and salt into a large bowl. Make a well in the centre, pour in the olive oil and the hand-hot water and mix to make a soft dough. Add more water if the dough looks a little dry. Knead for a couple of minutes or until smooth, wrap in clingfilm and leave to rest at room temperature for 30 minutes.

Divide the dough into 8, keeping the pieces covered under a large upturned bowl. Roll each into a thin 20-cm disc. Stack these up with non-stick baking paper or clingfilm between each, and cover with clingfilm or a damp tea towel.

Heat the testo on the hob until medium hot. Slide a disc of dough onto the hot testo and cook for about 30–40 seconds until brown spots appear on the underside. Flip it over and cook for a further 30 seconds or until both sides are dry-looking and covered with brown spots or blisters (like a Mexican tortilla or Indian chappati). Avoid cooking them for too long as they will end up being dry and tough.

Keep the cooked piadine warm and soft inside a folded napkin or loosely wrapped in foil in a warm oven, while you are cooking the remainder. They are best served warm and eaten on the same day.

This Ligurian speciality should be made with very good olive oil. It is traditionally baked in a large, shallow copper pan, but a wide metal pizza pan will do. The batter itself can be flavoured with chopped rosemary needles, dried chilli or black pepper. If you can't find Italian chickpea flour, use Indian gram flour (available in Asian food stores) although the colour will be paler.

# chickpea and rosemary flatbread

4 tablespoons extra virgin olive oil

200 g Italian chickpea flour (*farina di ceci*) or Indian gram flour

1 teaspoon fine sea salt

needles from 4 fresh rosemary sprigs

sea salt flakes and cracked black pepper, to sprinkle

*a pizza pan or shallow cake tin, 28 cm diameter, preferably non-stick*

makes 1 large flatbread

Put 500 ml cold water in a bowl with 1 tablespoon of the olive oil. Gradually whisk in the chickpea flour and fine sea salt until smooth and creamy. Cover and leave to stand for at least 30 minutes, or overnight in the refrigerator if possible.

Preheat the oven to 230°C (450°F) Gas 8.

Grease the pizza pan with the remaining olive oil. It must be well oiled to give the right flavour and ensure a crisp edge.

Stir the batter and pour it into the prepared pizza pan. Sprinkle the rosemary on top and bake for about 20 minutes or until set and golden.

Serve warm, cut into slices or lozenge shapes, and sprinkled with salt flakes and cracked black pepper. Best eaten on the same day.

# savoury bites

These little flatbreads are made with cornmeal and wheat flour. They are similar to English muffins and are served at local festivals in the Lunigiana, Tuscany. Cooked on a girdle and ready in minutes, they are golden and puffy, and smell delicious. Serve split and filled with cheese, alongside a selection of cold meats and salami.

# cornmeal muffins

25 g fresh yeast, 1 tablespoon dried active baking yeast or 2 teaspoons fast-action dried yeast

1 teaspoon sugar

400 ml hand-hot water

500 g Italian '00' flour or plain white flour

200 g fine cornmeal or polenta

1½ teaspoons fine sea salt

6 tablespoons extra virgin olive oil

*a testo or heavy-based frying pan*

makes 8 muffins

In a bowl, cream the fresh yeast with the sugar and whisk in the hand-hot water. Leave for about 10 minutes until frothy. For dried yeast, follow the manufacturer's instructions. Sift the flour, cornmeal and salt into a large bowl and make a well in the centre. Pour in the yeast mixture and olive oil. Mix together with a round-bladed knife, then your hands, until the dough comes together.

Tip the dough out onto a lightly-floured work surface, wash and dry your hands, then knead the dough briskly for 5–10 minutes until smooth, shiny and elastic – 5 minutes for warm hands, 10 minutes for cold hands! Try not to add any extra flour at this stage – a wetter dough is better. If you feel the dough is sticky, flour your hands and not the dough. The dough should be quite soft. If it is really too soft to handle, knead in a little more flour.

To test if the dough is ready, roll it into a fat sausage, take each end in either hand, lift the dough up and pull and stretch the dough outwards, gently wiggling it up and down – it should stretch out quite easily. If it doesn't, it needs more kneading. Shape into a neat ball. Put in an oiled bowl, cover with clingfilm or a damp tea towel and leave to rise in a warm place until doubled in size – about 1½ hours. Heat the testo or heavy-based frying pan on the hob until medium hot.

Uncover the dough, punch out the air, then tip out onto a lightly-floured work surface. Divide into 8 smooth balls, then flatten each into a disc about 1 cm thick. Slide 2 or 3 discs onto the hot testo or frying pan and cook for about 2 minutes on each side until risen and deep brown on the underside. Keep the cooked muffins warm and soft in a folded napkin or loosely wrapped in foil in a warm oven while cooking the rest. They are best served warm and eaten on the same day.

Almost like little muffins, these tiny treats hide a surprise when you bite into them – a cherry tomato bathed in pesto and melting mozzarella. Make them in advance and when you are ready to enjoy them, reheat in a warm oven.

# little stuffed focaccia muffins

½ recipe Deep-Pan Focaccia (page 21), making just 1 ball of dough, risen twice but uncooked

8 tablespoons fresh pesto

1 ball of mozzarella, squeezed of excess water and diced

24 small cherry tomatoes

olive oil, for brushing

a few fresh thyme or rosemary sprigs, to garnish

coarse sea salt or rock salt, to sprinkle

*a round biscuit cutter, 7 cm diameter (optional)*
*2 x 12-hole mini-muffin tins, oiled*

makes about 24 muffins

Preheat the oven to 200°C (400°F) Gas 6.

Uncover the dough, punch out the air and divide it into 4 pieces. Roll or pull each piece as thinly as you can on a well-floured work surface.

Using a biscuit cutter or an upturned glass, stamp out 6 small circles from the dough. Place a teaspoon of pesto in the middle of each circle, add a little mozzarella, then top with a cherry tomato. Bring the sides up and over the tomato and pinch to seal. Repeat with the remaining dough and fill ingredients to make a total of 24 muffins.

Put the muffins, sealed-side down, in the prepared mini-muffin tins. Brush the tops with a little olive oil, push in a herb sprig and sprinkle with coarse sea salt.

Bake for 10–15 minutes until risen and cooked through. Tip out of the tins and eat warm, as a snack with drinks. Best eaten on the same day but can be reheated just before serving, if liked.

These coccoli ('little darlings'!) are a type of savoury doughnut flavoured with pancetta. I add lightly crushed fennel seeds, a flavouring that is very popular in Tuscany, especially with cured pork. Make sure they are piping hot and sprinkled liberally with coarse sea salt when you serve them. You can grind fennel seeds over them for a special finishing touch.

# pancetta and fennel puffs

200 ml milk

50 g pure lard, roughly chopped

40 g fresh yeast or a 7-g sachet fast-action dried yeast

400 g Italian '00' flour or plain white flour

a good pinch of fine sea salt

50 g pancetta, finely diced

1 teaspoon fennel seeds, lightly crushed

vegetable or olive oil, for deep-frying

coarse sea salt or rock salt, to sprinkle

*a deep-fat fryer*

makes 30-40 puffs

Put the milk and lard in a saucepan and heat gently until the lard has melted. Don't let the milk get too hot. Crumble in the fresh yeast (if using) and whisk until dissolved.

Sift the flour and the fine sea salt into a bowl and make a well in the centre. If you are using fast-action dried yeast, stir it into the flour now. Pour in the warm milk mixture and add the pancetta and fennel seeds. Mix to a soft dough, adding more flour, if necessary. Form into a ball, cover with clingfilm or a damp tea towel and leave to rise in a warm place for 2 hours or until doubled in size.

Heat the oil in a deep fat fryer to 180°C (350°F). A piece of stale bread dropped in should sizzle and turn golden in a few seconds.

Uncover the dough, punch out the air and knead for 1 minute. Pull off small walnut-sized pieces of dough, about 2 cm, and roll into rough balls. Fry in batches for about 2–3 minutes each, until pale brown and puffy.

Remove with a slotted spoon and drain on kitchen paper. Sprinkle with coarse sea salt and serve whilst still hot. Best eaten on the same day.

These crisp little circles of fried pizza dough topped with a blob of tomato sauce, mozzarella and fresh basil, are often served in bars in Naples with your aperitivi. Although best served straight from the pan, you can make the puffy pizza bases beforehand, let them cool and store in an airtight container. To reheat, put them in a preheated oven at 180°C (350°F) Gas 4 for 2–3 minutes, then add the toppings and serve. A wok makes a perfect fryer for these.

# little fried Neapolitan pizzas

½ recipe Basic Pizza Dough (page 18), making just 1 ball of dough

200 ml any tomato pizza sauce

1 ball of mozzarella, squeezed of excess water and cut into tiny sticks

12 fresh basil leaves

vegetable or olive oil, for deep-frying

a round biscuit cutter, 5 cm diameter (optional)
a wok or deep-fat fryer

makes about 12 mini pizzas

Uncover the dough, punch out the air and roll or pull it very thinly on a well-floured surface. Using a biscuit cutter or an upturned glass, stamp out 12 or more 5-cm circles.

Heat the oil in a wok or deep-fat fryer to 190°C (375°F) or until a tiny piece of dough sizzles instantly when dropped in. Deep-fry the pizzas, 4 at a time, for 2–3 minutes or until puffed and golden. You will have to turn them now and again so that they colour evenly. Remove with a slotted spoon and drain well on kitchen paper.

Top with a little tomato sauce, a stick of mozzarella and a basil leaf. Best served immediately whilst still hot.

These tiny rounds of dough, flavoured with chopped spring onions or sun-dried tomatoes or herbs, are made and baked in minutes. Serve as a nibble with drinks or a starter, with olives, salami, prosciutto, soft cheese and your favourite selection of antipasti from the Italian deli.

# little spring onion breads

125 g self-raising white flour

¼ teaspoon fine sea salt

2 spring onions, finely chopped

2 tablespoons olive oil

1 large egg

2 teaspoons sesame seeds

freshly ground black pepper

*a round biscuit cutter,*
*5 cm diameter (optional)*

*a baking tray, lightly greased*

makes 12 very small rolls

Preheat the oven to 190°C (375°F) Gas 5.

In a large bowl, mix the flour with the salt, 3 grinds of pepper and the spring onions. In a separate bowl, whisk the olive oil with the egg and 1 tablespoon water, then add to the dry ingredients. Work the mixture with your hands to make a soft dough. If there are dry crumbs in the bowl, add more water 1 teaspoon at a time.

Turn the dough out onto a lightly-floured work surface and knead for 10 seconds to make a smooth ball. Cover with a damp tea towel and leave for a couple of minutes. Knead for a couple more seconds, then roll out to about 5 mm thickness. Stamp out rounds with a biscuit cutter or an upturned glass and set slightly apart on a baking tray. Gather up the trimmings and re-roll them, then cut out more rounds. Sprinkle with the sesame seeds and bake for 8–10 minutes or until golden brown and firm to the touch.

Serve warm from the oven. Best eaten the same day but can be frozen for up to 1 month. Thaw and gently reheat before serving.

variation:
Omit the spring onions and use either 1 rounded tablespoon chopped sun-dried tomatoes or 1 tablespoon snipped chives or freshly chopped flat leaf parsley.

# grissini and crisp breads

Schiacciata is a dialect word meaning 'flattened', so pizza is sometimes known as schiacciata, i.e. a flattened bread dough. After making pizza one day, I had some dough left over and devised this 'pizza' using leftover olives. There is no olive oil needed here, but you can have some really good olive oil in a little pot ready for dipping the hot pizzas into.

# crispy olive 'pizza'

1 recipe Basic Pizza Dough (page 18) or any leftover dough

a splash of white wine

a handful of green olives, stoned and roughly chopped

coarse sea salt or rock salt, to sprinkle

extra virgin olive oil, to serve

*a testo, terracotta bakestone or a large, heavy baking tray*

*a large, rimless baking tray*

makes about 20-25 pieces

Put the testo, terracotta bakestone or a large, heavy baking tray on the lower shelf of the oven. Preheat the oven to 220°C (425°F) Gas 7 for at least 30 minutes.

Uncover the dough and punch out the air. Using a rolling pin, roll the dough out as thinly as you can, directly onto the baking tray. Brush the surface with a little white wine, scatter with the olives and sprinkle with coarse sea salt. Lightly press the olives and salt into the dough. Using a pizza wheel, score the dough in lozenge shapes directly on the baking tray.

Bake for 5–10 minutes, until puffed and pale golden. Remove from the oven and break up into the pre-cut lozenges. Serve warm with olive oil for dipping and drizzling.

I bought a factory-produced version of this in Tuscany and it inspired me to bake my own.
It's so easy to make that you quickly get into the rhythm of preparing it until it becomes
second nature. Use any leftover dough that you might have.

# crispy pizza sheets

1 recipe Basic Pizza Dough
(page 18) or any leftover dough

2 teaspoons dried rosemary
(optional)

extra virgin olive oil, to glaze

sea salt flakes, to sprinkle

2 large, heavy baking trays,
lightly oiled

makes about 6 large pieces

Preheat the oven to 230°C (450°F) Gas 8.

Uncover the dough, punch out the air and knead in the dried rosemary
(if using). Divide the dough into 6 pieces and roll or pull it directly onto the
prepared baking trays. Press it out with your fingers as large and flat as you
can. The dough should be so thin you can almost see through it – and it
doesn't have to be even.

Brush it lightly with olive oil and scatter with sea salt flakes. Bake for about
8 minutes until golden, lightly bubbled, dry and crisp. Shatter the sheets
like poppadoms to serve.

We all know the paper packets containing a couple of grissini (breadsticks) which many Italian restaurants serve, but these are a more sophisticated version and can be made using leftover pizza dough. Just knead in the black pepper or any other flavouring that takes your fancy.

# peppered grissini

½ recipe Basic Pizza Dough (page 18), making just 1 ball of dough

2 tablespoons cracked black pepper

2 tablespoons extra virgin olive oil

25 g butter, melted

*a baking tray, lightly greased*

makes about 20 breadsticks

Make the pizza dough according to the recipe on page 18, adding the cracked pepper to the ingredients. Mix the olive oil and melted butter together. Before the first rising, roll or pull the dough into a thin rectangle, brush all over with the olive oil and butter mixture and roll up loosely like a Swiss roll. Flatten with the palm of your hand, then lift it onto a floured work surface, cover with clingfilm and leave to rise for 30 minutes.

Preheat the oven to 200°C (400°F) Gas 6.

Flatten the risen dough with your hand again to knock out the air, then roll out to a thickness of 5 mm. Cut into long, thin strips and twist like barley sugar. Lay these onto a baking tray and spray with water. Bake for 5 minutes, spray again, then bake for a further 10–15 minutes or until golden and crisp. Keep an eye on them while they are baking as they can burn. Leave to cool on a wire rack and store in an airtight container for up to 1 week.

In Ligurian dialect, a ciappa is a thin, flat stone that has been used for baking flatbreads since the dawn of time. Nowadays these stones, made from a type of slate, are used to cook meat and fish at the table. A ciappa can also mean a slate roof tile, and has come to mean a thin, crisply baked savoury biscuit, reminiscent of the shape of these ancient Ligurian roof tiles.

# ciappe 'roof tiles'

1 tablespoon fine sea salt

100 ml hand-hot water

250 g Italian '00' flour or plain white flour

2 tablespoons extra virgin olive oil

*2 large, heavy baking trays*

makes about 10 pieces

In a bowl, mix the salt with the warm water until dissolved. Sift the flour into a medium bowl and make a well in the centre. Pour in the salty water and olive oil. Mix well, then knead the dough lightly for a couple of minutes until it is smooth. The dough should be firmer than pizza dough. Wrap it in clingfilm and leave to rest for 15 minutes.

Preheat the oven to 180°C (350°F) Gas 4.

Divide the dough into 8. Roll or pull the pieces into long ovals. Roll them as thinly as you can (a couple of millimetres) and keep the work surface well floured to prevent sticking. Alternatively, you can use a pasta machine to roll them out if you are making a large quantity.

Lay the tiles on the baking trays and prick all over with a fork with large tines. Make sure they are liberally peppered with holes.

Bake for 15–20 minutes or until evenly pale golden and dried out. Leave to cool on a wire rack and store in an airtight container for up to 2 weeks.

For all you anchovy-lovers out there, these are just the job. Transform leftover pizza dough into a savoury snack by flavouring it with anchovies. The combination of these simple twists and a glass of chilled white wine truly transports you to a sunny terrace in southern Italy.

# anchovy twists

½ recipe Basic Pizza Dough
(page 18), making
just 1 ball of dough

50 g tinned anchovies in oil,
drained and chopped

vegetable or olive oil,
for deep-frying

coarse sea salt or rock salt and
cracked black pepper, to sprinkle

*a wok or deep-fat fryer*

makes about 15–20 twists

Uncover the dough, punch out the air and knead in the anchovies. Roll or pull the dough out thinly and cut into long rectangles with a crinkled pastry wheel or a sharp knife. Make a slash in the middle of each rectangle, bring one end up and push through the slit, pulling it through loosely to make a roughly twisted shape.

Heat the oil in a wok or deep fat fryer to 190°C (375°F) and deep-fry the twists in batches until golden and crisp. Remove with a slotted spoon and drain on kitchen paper. Sprinkle with coarse sea salt and cracked pepper and serve warm.

The twists can be stored in an airtight container for up to 1 week. Reheat them for a few minutes in a warm oven when you are ready to enjoy them.

# sweet breads

This is a rich, sweet, light-textured Italian breakfast bread flavoured with oranges. It is made with pine nuts and hazelnuts in Southern Italy and with almonds in Sardinia. The nuts are gently toasted for maximum flavour.

# pignola

100 g sultanas

the grated zest and freshly squeezed juice of 2 unwaxed oranges

400 g unbleached strong white bread flour

1 teaspoon fine sea salt

150 g unsalted butter, diced

2 eggs, beaten

2 tablespoons hand-hot water

15 g fresh yeast*

30 g hazelnuts, lightly toasted in a dry frying pan

100 g pine nuts, lightly toasted in a dry frying pan

icing sugar, for dusting

*a baking tray, well greased*

### makes 1 large loaf

* To use fast-action dried yeast, mix a 7 g sachet with the flour after the butter has been rubbed in. Add the eggs and sultana mixture plus 2 tablespoons water; then continue as in the main recipe.

Put the sultanas, orange zest and juice in a bowl and let soak overnight.

Next day, mix the flour and salt in a large bowl. Rub the diced butter into the flour with the tips of your fingers until the mixture looks like coarse breadcrumbs. Make a well in the centre, then add the beaten eggs and the soaked sultana mixture.

Put the hand-hot water in a bowl, crumble the yeast over the top and mix to a smooth liquid. Pour into the well in the flour. Mix the yeast, eggs and sultanas together in the well, then gradually work in the flour to make a very soft, slightly sticky dough. If there are dry crumbs in the bowl, or the dough seems dry and tough, work in a little more hand-hot water, 1 tablespoon at a time.

Turn the dough out onto a floured work surface. Knead for 5 minutes. It will be soft and pliable but not as sticky. Return it to the bowl, cover with clingfilm and leave to rise in a warm place until doubled in size, about 3 hours.

Turn the risen dough out onto a floured work surface, sprinkle with the nuts and gently work them in. When they are evenly distributed, shape the dough into a ball, then pat into a round about 20 cm diameter and 3.5 cm thick. Set on the prepared baking tray. Slip the tray into a large plastic bag, inflate slightly, seal, then leave to rise in a warm place until doubled in size, about 1 hour. Allow longer if the dough has been in the refrigerator.

Preheat the oven to 190°C (375°F) Gas 5.

Uncover the dough and bake for 35 minutes or until the loaf is golden brown and sounds hollow when tapped underneath. Transfer to a wire rack, dust with icing sugar and leave to cool. Eat within 4 days or wrap in foil and freeze for up to 1 month.

This is a delicious bread to serve warm from the oven at breakfast time. I've used fresh black grapes here, but I have also made a lovely version using semi-dried Montepulciano grapes. If you wanted to try something similar, you could substitute semi-dried cherries or plump Lexia raisins. Serve it with salty cheeses such as Gorgonzola or Parmesan.

# black grape schiacciata

80 ml extra virgin olive oil

a handful of fresh rosemary needles

450 g extra strong white bread flour

1 teaspoon fine sea salt

2 tablespoons caster sugar

1 teaspoon fast-action dried yeast

250 ml hand-hot water

400 g seedless black grapes

*a deep baking tin, oiled*

makes 1 medium loaf

Put the olive oil and rosemary in a bowl. Give the rosemary several good squeezes to release the aroma into the oil. Set aside for a few minutes.

Put the flour, salt and 1 tablespoon of the sugar in a large bowl and stir well. Add the yeast and stir again. Pour in 2 tablespoons of the infused, strained olive oil and enough hand-hot water to make a soft but not sticky dough.

Turn the dough out on to a lightly-floured work surface and knead for 5 minutes, until the dough is smooth and elastic. Fold in the grapes and knead for a further 2–3 minutes. The dough may become sticky at this point, so dust with a little extra flour if necessary.

Press the dough into the prepared baking tin and push it with your knuckles to fill the tin. Leave to rise in a warm place for about 40 minutes, or until it has doubled in size. Preheat the oven to 220°C (425°F) Gas 7.

Drizzle the remaining infused olive oil over the risen dough and scatter some of the rosemary needles and the remaining sugar evenly across the top. Bake for about 25 minutes or until the surface is golden brown and the base sounds hollow when tapped. Cool on a wire rack.

Eat on the same day or let cool completely, wrap in foil and freeze. When you remove the bread from the freezer, thaw and wrap in foil, then reheat for 5 minutes in a hot oven.

This bread is delicious toasted for breakfast. Rather than spreading it with butter, try serving it with a sort of dressing which I make by whisking a little hazelnut oil and honey together with some orange zest. The bread is also lovely served with soft cream cheese.

# fig and hazelnut breakfast bread

500 g strong white bread flour

2 teaspoons fine sea salt

50 g caster sugar

a 7-g sachet fast-action dried yeast

2 tablespoons hazelnut oil

200 ml hand-hot water

2 tablespoons blanched hazelnuts, toasted and chopped

300 g ready-to-eat dried figs, quartered

*2 baking trays, oiled*

makes 2 small loaves

Sift the flour and salt into a large bowl and stir in the sugar. Add the yeast and stir again. Pour in the hazelnut oil and enough hand-hot water to make a soft but not sticky dough. Add the hazelnuts and figs and knead well to combine.

Turn the dough out onto a lightly-floured work surface and knead for 5–10 minutes. Divide into two rough loaves and put on the prepared baking trays. Leave to rise in a warm place for about 1 hour, or until the dough has doubled in size.

Preheat the oven to 220°C (425°F) Gas 7.

Cut a couple of slashes in the top of each loaf and bake for about 25–30 minutes, until golden and firm and the bases sound hollow when tapped. Cool on a wire rack.

Eat on the same day or let cool completely, wrap in foil and freeze. When you remove the bread from the freezer, thaw and wrap in foil, then reheat for 5 minutes in a hot oven.

Mixing wheat flour with chestnut flour gives this bread a wonderful sweet and savoury flavour that's almost smoky. It is generally made during the autumn or winter months when chestnut flour is readily available. Serve it with Gorgonzola and pears and extra Vin Santo, of course.

# chestnut and Vin Santo focaccia

500 g Italian '00' flour or plain white flour

200 g chestnut flour (*farina di castagne*)

1 teaspoon fine sea salt

25 g fresh yeast, 1 tablespoon dried active yeast or 2 teaspoons fast-action dried yeast

150 ml extra virgin olive oil

150 ml Vin Santo mixed with 300 ml water, warmed

coarse sea salt or rock salt, to sprinkle

*2 cake tins, pie or pizza pans, 25 x 4 cm, lightly oiled*

makes 2 focaccias

Sift both the flours and fine sea salt into a large bowl and make a well in the centre. Crumble in the fresh yeast. For dried yeast, follow the manufacturer's instructions.

Pour in 3 tablespoons of the olive oil, then rub the oil into the flour and yeast until the mixture resembles fine breadcrumbs. Pour the warmed Vin Santo and water into the well and mix until the dough comes together.

Tip out onto a lightly-floured work surface, wash and dry your hands, then knead the dough briskly for 10 minutes until smooth and elastic. The dough should be very soft, almost too soft to handle, but don't worry at this stage. Put in a lightly-oiled bowl, cover with clingfilm or a damp tea towel and leave to rise in a warm place until doubled in size – about 1½ hours.

Uncover the dough, punch out the air, then divide into 2. Shape each piece into a round ball on a lightly-floured work surface. Roll out into two 25-cm circles and put in the tins. Cover with clingfilm or a damp tea towel and leave to rise in a warm place for about 45 minutes or until very puffy and almost risen to the top of the tins.

Uncover the dough and, using your fingertips, make deep dimples all over the surface of the dough right to the base of the tin. Drizzle over the remaining olive oil, re-cover and leave to rise for a final 30 minutes.

Preheat the oven to 200°C (400°F) Gas 6.

Spray the focaccias with water, lightly sprinkle with coarse sea salt and bake for 20–25 minutes, until risen and golden. Transfer to a wire rack to cool. Eat on the same day or let cool completely, wrap in foil and freeze. When you remove the bread from the freezer, thaw and wrap in foil, then reheat for 5 minutes in a hot oven.

# index

## recipe credits

All recipes by **Maxine Clark** except:

**Linda Collister**

Ciabatta rolls
Little spring onion breads
Pignola
Tuscan fresh sage and olive oil bread

**Liz Franklin**

Black grape schiacciata
Fig and hazelnut breakfast bread

## photography credits

All photography by **Richard Jung** except:

**Martin Brigdale**

Pages 1 inset, 2, 15 and 56.

**Peter Cassidy**

Page 6 left.

**Kate Whitaker**

Pages 1 background, 5 right, 6–7 background, 7 below left, 9, 12, 21, 37, 44, 47 and 57.